D1081049

RAIDING THE BORDERS

MARION LOMAX

◉

Raiding the Borders

BLOODAXE BOOKS

Copyright © Marion Lomax 1996

ISBN: 1 85224 352 X

First published 1996 by
Bloodaxe Books Ltd,
P.O. Box 1SN,
Newcastle upon Tyne NE99 1SN.

Bloodaxe Books Ltd acknowledges
the financial assistance of Northern Arts.

LEGAL NOTICE

All rights reserved. No part of this book may be
reproduced, stored in a retrieval system, or
transmitted in any form, or by any means, electronic,
mechanical, photocopying, recording or otherwise,
without prior written permission from Bloodaxe Books Ltd.

Requests to publish work from this book
must be sent to Bloodaxe Books Ltd.

Marion Lomax has asserted her right under
Section 77 of the Copyright, Designs and Patents Act 1988
to be identified as the author of this work.

Cover printing by J. Thomson Colour Printers Ltd, Glasgow.

Printed in Great Britain by
Cromwell Press Ltd, Broughton Gifford, Melksham, Wiltshire.

for all my family –
on both sides of the border

ACKNOWLEDGEMENTS

Acknowledgements are due to the editors of the following publications in which some of these poems (or versions of them) first appeared: *Aquarius, Klaonica: poems for Bosnia* (Bloodaxe Books / The Independent, 1993), *New Poetry, The Oxford Magazine, Poetry Review, Poetry Wales, Poetry with an Edge* (Bloodaxe Books, 1993), *Sixty Women Poets* (Bloodaxe Books, 1993), *Strawberry Fare, The Times Literary Supplement* and *Writing Women*. Three of these poems were the basis for a libretto, *Beyond Men and Dreams*, which was commissioned by the Royal Opera House and performed as part of the 1991 Garden Venture (composer: Bennett Hogg).

Marion Lomax was awarded a Hawthornden Fellowship in 1993: grateful thanks are due to Drew Heinz and to the Administrators of Hawthornden Castle.

The cover picture, *A Leningrad Woman* (1983-5) by O.K. Yakhnin, was shown in the exhibition 'Back in the USSR' in 1994-95. Thanks are due to the Laing Art Gallery and photographers OMG in Newcastle upon Tyne for their assistance, and to the Central House of Artists, Moscow, for their kind permission to reproduce the painting.

CONTENTS

DIFFICULT TIMES

BORDERS

Kith

On the other side of the border
they call this *Scozia Irredenta*:
unredeemed.
       A few coffers of coins
didn't change hands; a battle was lost
instead of won; the in-between land
stays in-between.
       A line on a map
moved back through the years
          down to the Tees.
England was never an only child
but has grown to think so. Stone streets dip –
rise. They're burning coal on morning fires
in dark front rooms: smoke gusts over roofs.
Gardens, late coming into flower,
brazen it out with bright aubrietia.

I've followed the hills to Carter Bar
past lost peels, and moors where soaking sheep
stagger between tufts of died-back grass.
Standing in the rain, she's there – harassed,
hurt – a foster-mother, telling me
she hasn't much to offer. I'll take
my chance: I don't believe her.
          The bends
on the border
       won't make up their minds.
Five times
       they twist me round, but I still
head north.

Compass

From the back yard look across the valley:
the Tyne winds east past castle and factory,
imperceptibly tidal. If you live
here long enough you learn to sense changes
as surreptitious as the river's ebb.

Once it was easier to keep your bearings –
the West Road to Hexham, the old East School;
though I lived in South Road the view was north,
child and woman before me would look up,
eyes drawn over fields to the Cheviots.

We were rivers who flowed from west to east,
to work and school, who faced north when we stopped
because it was known. Yet at our backs there was
always the south, enjoying the most sun,
making the needle quiver, faces turn.

Sealing

(for my Arran cousins)

It is evening on Arran, antlers on a sky-line
as the mountain gathers its ridge of eyes, shy of us,
and soon gone – like this memory my mind fails to hold
four hundred miles south, far from the sea and scent of seals.

I am struggling free, feel the hard floor shrink to pebbles.
My feet deep in shingle, waves break on the other side
of the window, and I wait – wait until it seems that
the sea flows into a field, an edge of dry garden.

Then just when my soles sense the smoothness of boards, they slip
and I see the first dark head far out in the water –
another, another. I call them to swim closer
where roses bloom in plankton, to wash me from this room.

Before sand settles on a faded Persian carpet
a pup dives into its green and magenta. The wools
grow luminous underwater. Fish flick from nowhere
round my chair legs. Currents are colder than expected.

I swim off a shore-line sheltered by Kintyre: it is
late evening on Arran. I have been here a long time,
sleep seal sleep, swallow squid and eels – days brimming lust as
land trees ripen – watch humans safely from a distance.

Between Voyages

You brought me a seahorse, succulent shells.
The boat in the garden nudges the hedge;
its shrouds call up storms and a distant sea
where people, like sails, flap impatiently
with the pain of the land-bound watching tides.

Rain skitters down tiles: the gutters have gone.
Water flows below floors, rises up through
the ground floating spring bulbs and snails; their shells
striped whorls, brittle as memories of your voice –
close as the cold day, dark as our lost north.

I savour the sea horse, stroke a starfish
I once found – stiff-fingered in the sea coal
of a wintered town. All day, through the house,
I have shells beneath my feet. The floors give
and flood, gulls wheel above this inland roof.

First Lessons

I have learnt to walk
with fear on a leash:
it used to snarl at the door
every time I tried to leave.
Now it trots quietly
on impacted earth,
and sometimes it sleeps.

I'd forgotten how minds
can be open to the sky
with no overhanging boulders –
what it feels like to lie
stretched in damp, warm grass
with insects in my hair –
and the way you can hear
minute thrusts of plants.

I have perfected
throwing anger to gulls
who mew it back to sea,
and I marvel that sleep
saunters down from the high trees
to spirit you up there –
leaving the room without
opening a window.

Gruoch Considers

Dochter tae a king, faither sin taen,
mairrit, sin weeda. Aa dinna greet.
Ma lad, Lulach, maun gang hes ain gait
an gie's ane bricht chance tae lauch agin.
Nae weeda gin wife. Aa'm a steekit yett
sae bleth'rin gabs canna ca' 'Bizzem'.
It's sair ta dae – wha winna fa' whiles?
Aa'm youthfu' an maun hae a man sune
ellis ma saul sall skirl. Aa munna smuir.

MacBeathain cam yestreen. Dander lass,
ye winna swither an baith say ay.
Daith is aye ahint yon spaywife. Juist
tak wha ye wad – MacBeathain, Macbeth.

Gruoch

I have a name of my own. Gruoch –
a low growl of desire. He'd say it
and crush me against his throat. Gruoch –
his huge hands stroking my hip-length hair,
grasping it in his fists, drawing it taut
either side of my arms in ropes,
staked like a tent. He'd gasp when
folds slipped open, succulent
as split stems, to welcome him in.
How I held him, squeezed the sorrow
of no son out of him – for Lulach
was only mine, fruit of first union –
of Gillecomgain, forgotten by time.

He brought me Duncan as a trophy,
sweet revenge for my father's slaughter.
Upstarts never prosper. I was the true
King's daughter, Gruoch – uttered in wonder.
Seventeen years we reigned together through
keen seasons of hunger, feasting one to other.
War nor wantons wrenched him from me:
Gruoch – a whisper, sustaining fire.

He died before the battle with Malcolm:
obsequics cradled in a dry bed.
My mouth meandered down his body –
but it was winter, no bud stirring.
Gruoch – despairing: our death rattle.

Quaking Houses
(in memory of Elizabeth and Arthur Gowland)

I still remember the sound of your laugh,
the lift of the latch; this is how lives pass.
There'd be a fire roaring in the range,
pans on trivets hissing into the flames,
and you'd roll a live coal across your hand
(underground, you'd nearly lost the whole arm):
'See this, pet!' 'Arthur, leave the bairn alone.'

Pit-wheel at the end of the street, high wall –
the same pit-head pool where you sat the night
my mother was born, keeping 'out the way'
as you'd been told. Listening to a vixen
bark across the fells, hunting for her young –
you thought of your hens, Lizzie's oaths, her moans.
Groped in the May dark for a woman's voice
that would let you go home. The midwife burnt
newspapers soaked in blood; you kissed Lizzie
on the lips, stroked my mother's face with a
finger betraying a trace of coal, though
you'd scrubbed your hands till they were almost raw.

She slept, your child; the house was quiet then.
Soon it quaked twice more with a mother's screams;
stairs and rooms strained as the three of them grew,
pounding the gently sinking floors; struggling
with doors that wouldn't close, dropped in their frames.
Windows stuck; the walls were shifting their weight
every time part of a ceiling collapsed
in a tunnel hundreds of feet beneath.

War lit its own fires, the sky flared for miles;
planes whined past: 'As if it's not worth bombing.'
Tending your allotment, feeding your hens,
you watched Italian prisoners cross the fells.
Just two of you now, you'd saved a few pounds
to move from the street to a 'proper' town
but Lizzie died of cancer   you'd retired.
Silicosis, heart; you had a few years.

The houses? Modernised, without the mine,
they're still standing firm at thousands a time –
I can hear you laugh. This is how lives pass.

The Advance

The morning mist sprouts phantom trees. I see
you against them, using a rake to scythe
shoulder-high saplings which edge our garden.
Fields clear between your arm and the horizon,
where the fields have retreated – lining up
at a distance, still holding back vapour.
Inside that bulky whiteness skulk shadows
of about-to-be-built houses. The fields
seem to shrink behind you. Damp air muffles
voices – future arguments – their children.

In the newly-exposed garden I call
birdsong closer, plant hedges of roses.
A passing horse trips, hooves rebalancing;
rabbits twitch in the field, run for cover.
Age, like the mist, creeps ever nearer, yet
tenderly we hug this house around us.
My hair is stiff with dust: you don't notice –
silver glints in a tendril: you stroke it.

Forgotten Feast

From the lodge a narrow, railed way
bisects bored sheep who nibble time
back to the eighteenth-century house.
A crescent sweeps below the steps
and plane trees wait until we pass
to let some tenuously joined leaves
finally sever stems and fall.

Then, you would not have held my hand –
you might have offered me your arm.
We would have strolled, but never kissed
in full view of late-flowering shrubs
and if our fingers dared to touch
on pretext – you would stroke my glove.
We might, however, *talk* of love.

'Bodies respond to pheromones.
A child's first smile is just a trick
to bond its mother – and our minds
manipulate what we can find
by way of feelings, to survive.'
Kiss me. We're moving between times:
we have a chance to redefine.

Pianos stand in empty rooms
caught in a long extended pause,
dressed for dinner, but no one dines.
Make the old maze negotiable
so by the ice-house at the lake
fresh footsteps leave our clear imprint.
Tip back the melted years and drink.

Somewhere Else

When I phone part of me listens for home
hidden behind you: sometimes a cat purrs
from your knee. Here, you'll just hear my TV –
switched on so that something moves in the room.

We strangle feelings, squeezing them down wires.
My feet seek you in the night, my hands search
between cold sheets, and I wake confused with
windows in new places, the wardrobe moved.

Though not properly awake, already
I'm tuned in to the sound of distant planes.
As I staunch the sense of a severed self,
I feel you move silently, somewhere else.

This Time

I thought it came through the window
but, of course, that wasn't open.
Moments before, dogs were barking,
house by house, as they sensed it pass.
Something scrabbled in the wood pile
where pieces of unfinished boat
lay till they could be given life.
You were still sleeping beside me,
never noticed it drag me out,
fastened to the top of my back.

The conscious mind hissed 'Squirrel...claws',
but I could feel tiny fingers
rifling my hair, knuckles against
the nape of my neck as I fell.
I heard it cry once and knew then
that its name was the same as yours –
yet you would never defend it.
Awake, you might just have killed it,
thrown it out, taken me to bed,
and helped to soothe subsequent dreams.

Ullambana

My strong spirit
we are in this together,
let us take to the streets
like all the others –
though the night,
alight with lanterns,
will not lead us
to a family.

Around us, ancestors
seek descendants.
On every street corner
we see a mother
claimed by a daughter,
a father embraced
by a weeping son.
We never made tears
for anyone.

While monks recite
their sacred verses,
souls are locked
inside houses,
finding that they
don't like the changes;
that it's only ritual
making them welcome.

No one has made
an offering to us:
faithful spirit,
take this presence –
dance closer
than bodies let us.
We expect nothing,
can't be disappointed.

Boats are burning
down the river:
dark birds of tissue
whirl through us.
My strong spirit
we are in this together,
just your soul, my soul,
more loyal than children.

Raiding the Borders

Limmer thieves from robber towers,
the reivers rode after Lammas
when nights were longest, horses stronger.
Sometimes those they sought to plunder
saw the fires lit in warning,
heard the fray bell, were prepared.

Centuries later feuds were buried,
families allied to survive.
As my mother met my father,
back through the Bolams and the Halls,
Rutherfords, and Burnses further north –
marriages crossed over borders.

When they came down from the shires
the auld Halls settled by the Tyne
in a home the Percies gave them.
Walls a yard deep like a stronghold,
for the proud hill a proud cottage –
and we stayed two hundred years.

The line grew through generations:
six children, nine, then eleven.
Grandmother, the eldest daughter,
a widow at twenty-seven –
sixty years without her husband –
taught me how to live with borders.

When she crossed I could not follow,
but learnt how silent some raids were.
By twenty I knew treachery;
a friend, a sister was stolen
in the dark months of winter
then, after a long siege, my father.

We are never free from borders.
My mother died on an ocean,
shores at its reaches; no fixed limits,
just sea reclaiming then retreating.
the house was empty of all it guarded:
another raid had been unexpected.

We meet now on debatable land –
neither south nor north, but beyond both –
and in those moments everywhere
is full of her – the sky, the sun
as it falls by an open door –
she's before me throughout the house.

In the air I feel her pity
for the way we let rooms trap us;
the need we have to put up walls
and defend them; the fear we make
for each other by warring raids
which haste us to that last border.

When I surrendered their old home
I dreamt one night they all came back,
waved to me, walking down the path –
five generations who had striven
to keep the house their parents left them.
If we can't defend we are forgiven.

Divided We Stand

You are looking at me now like the man from Special Branch
who scrutinised my face when I waited to board the plane.
I thought – somewhere there must be a terrorist with my eyes –
I expected to be stopped. He waved everyone straight through.

I came separate, out of place, through my own act of faith.
You stood among families waiting to be completed –
but I had never promised. Doubts soon sabotaged your smile.
Now we move from room to room switching on and off the lamps.

I wake before dawn. A bang: my bed is scattered with glass –
shards, glimmers, jagged pieces. The floor is sharp, clothes covered.
You fill the doorway, lift me; my feet touch down in your room –
'Keep right back from the window!' – but outside the street is calm.

An empty chair, a towel – your clothes are tidied away.
Only the bed is betrayed, the imprint of your body.
You do not declare your fear, your craving. No crucifix
clings to the wall, yet your eyes are praying into the dark.

At the side of the curtain we peer down to a pavement
which keeps its feet a secret under a stone-blinded lamp.
You are looking at me now as if you hope I'll declare
a shared religion or guilt, something that might help us cry.

The closed door has a halo. Shut out, shut in, it's the same.
You hold me pressed against you; pick the glass out of my hair.

AMOR DIVING

Mariamne Johnes of Hafod

Fathers love daughters.
I was never as strong
as he willed his care
to make me. I dreamed
a rare garden: he decreed
Mariamne in marble –
without means to pay the mason,
who would not release me.

My father's house burned:
my garden died. Paid for
at last, they carried me
through the long wet grass
to our family church.
Life was locked behind
cold, smooth eyes and
I could not smile.

Men kept their distance
from your marble daughter
until the roof sparks stung her –
I heard you, my father,
in their voices calling out
for water. They ran
with pitchers, any vessel
they could find to fill.

Rafters blazed and fell.
I glowed. Alone, I strained,
contained the red heat;
pitched my heart
to its highest note,
thinking of your love.
I could have withstood
anything but water.

I shattered when they threw
the first heavy sheet across.
The hiss and crack,
the scorching steam
drove them back, while shock
rent every invisible bone,
making your grief and my body
one, at the last, dear father.

Transliteration

(for Ann)

Twenty years ago at the moment my father died
I was trying to transliterate заканчивать,
had substituted more than half of it: ZAKANCHIV...
in capitals on top of a three-by-four buff card.
Like most things I did in those days, it made little sense.
I followed instructions; behaved as was expected –
filed Russian cards, drove north each weekend, watched him suffer
for two years while no one acknowledged he was dying –
wanted to risk truth but didn't dare to. Daily we
dragged an unspeakable secret around with our souls.
Then, the most apt word would have been страшный:
for him, for us, there was no sign of it finishing.

In those days, at work, my eyes read all words as Russian
whatever the language – so that today, when I hear
Mandelstam's poetry read by a woman whose name
I cannot catch, my mind lurches from the moon, a clock,
the clapping, crowded room, to the desk where I waited
every Friday afternoon before the long haul home,
desperate to translate the incomprehensible
into something which would allow me to bring comfort
to him, my mother, myself. Yet transliteration
was all that was asked of me – just the substitution
of sham for true letters – to form words we could handle,
but nothing that might ever make a living language.

Special Delivery

Daddy was tied like a parcel,
paper crept steadily round him;
festive with lilies and crucifix
we waited to fasten the string.

I wanted to try for an angel
but demand is high these days;
cheques are too easy, and the heart
hadn't enough small change.

Daddy was tissue paper;
ink stains smudged his eyes.
The wrapping folded over
but he didn't realise.

His room flapped white and yellow,
settling gold when we walked in,
and the angels sniffed at the window,
on the outside, looking thin.

I packed fine memories round him
as gently as I could.
Love, wrapped untold beside him
for fear he understood.

I could not loose the paper
holding him gagged and bound.
We both struggled against it
but it coiled more tightly round.

The angels, unasked, were refusing
to redirect him home,
so I wrote out the label –
'Daddy – destination unknown.'

Amor Diving

(for my mother)

After the police left, having told me of your death,
I picked up the mail I'd thrown on the table
when I came in. Your card slipped out to be read:
but it's not the words you sent me from Lisbon,
the hopes for a smoother voyage after Morocco,
or even your faithful promise to meet me
which stay most strongly – for I remember
the care you would take to choose each picture,
so that was where I first looked for an answer.

I thought the name on the boat you'd picked, bobbing
in the harbour, was *Amor Diving* – just as ours did
into difficult waters – though it always surfaced.
Later, before I sang them at your service,
I realised the words were *Amor Divino*.
For all our differences, that stubborn thread
I tugged at times and frayed, holds still and strengthens
with every passing day. You are proving to me
that no one will ever love me better, telling me
what neither of us ever managed to say.

The First Week

I have left your lipstick by the mirror,
your shoes on the first three rungs of stairs.
I have watered each fuchsia in the porch:
your cacti are flowering like red hands
reaching into the deep window
I would look through to see you
walking up the path.

Every day I make your bed,
sleep in it every night,
trying to dream you back –
but I can't hear your voice
and you stopped the clock yourself
before you left.

Today I started to open your mail,
rifled clothes for your scent
(which seems to grow stronger),
found the letter you wrote to my father
twelve years after he died.

The old mirror has melted
and run under the door, but you are
safe inside me. I will be your reflection:
out here facing the next thirty years.

Post-natal

Being a midwife, you were different
to other mothers, never fussed. You fed
and calmly cared for three generations
under the same roof.

My father once said he was heart-broken
when you left me in my cot, closed the door,
and told him I'd stop crying once I knew
you wouldn't come.

Lately, like a child, I've woken crying;
hungry to see you, touch you, talk to you.
I think you hear me in some far-off room,
would come now if you could.

We all have a second umbilical cord –
the one we never see, that is of our making.
It feeds comfort from wherever you are now;
do not cut it.

The Day of the Funeral

She was born and died in the same month – May,
chilly as it often is in the north.
In a way I felt I met her at the church,
could sense her relief at being home
after those last eventful weeks.
Clouds threatened as we came out of doors,
climbed into the long, silent hearse,
and followed her finally down the street
where she'd shopped for over forty years.

Out past the houses, banks of blazing gorse
flashed the sun she'd managed to switch on.
I felt her with me, yet outside the car.
At every turn of the road I loved her more,
wanted to cling to that part of her
under the red roses and polished wood;
could imagine her – tense, apprehensive,
tight-lipped – putting up with the whole business;
yet the warmth of her smile was everywhere.

The Other Itinerary

Dying's never easy:
you did the best you could –
sent me a card that arrived
the same day as the news;
made sure I had photos of you
smiling, right up to the last minute;
went out in style at a party –
quickly, quietly – in the calm Pacific.

Now, when your face
comes before me
you are usually laughing.
I feel us smiling together
at the death certificate
signed by the Russian doctor
with its 'Welcome aboard' motto
in the corner.

I worried that we'd finished
your film of holiday photos
taking pictures of the flowers
on your grave – then knew
you hadn't minded: it was
how it ended – the way
we welcomed you home.

Worse was the suitcase
I collected without you
but, even then, you hinted
you didn't really need it.
While others had specified
'being met', for once you'd written
just: 'own arrangements'.

Left Luggage

'You can't take it with you,' she used to say,
reading who'd left how much in the paper.
The house is sold but I dream her in it –
struggling through the door with bags and cases
more substantial than she is – leaving them
abandoned on the floor because there is
nowhere to put them.

Someone has filled her cupboards with their clothes.
I know she searches, but cannot see her;
can feel the frenzy in the air, her sense
of things removed, misplaced, not remembering
how, or why, or when. This is vaster than
all the small forgetfulnesses she'd been
used to while she lived.

It's as if time moved on months when she left,
instead of the two weeks she intended –
so that now she's returned, laden and tired,
her life has been wiped out in her absence.
We've sent her home to Oxfam or auctions;
absorbed it, in fragments, into our own:
allowed her to fade.

But in the dream I feel clearly; hear her
wondering why the telephone doesn't ring,
why a new family has changed her number.
And I call see all their puzzled faces
as, every morning, when they go downstairs,
they trip over more of her discarded
luggage.

July

Watching a different sea
to the one on which you died,
I try locking a curious gull
eye to eye.

I am with him on the roof's edge,
thinking only 'high water'.
Then, 'This time last year
I had a mother.'

It's as if one grief breeds others.
When we reached the cliff path
they'd just found the body.

After you died I felt nowhere was safe
but this familiar place
could have been the exception.

Last night I dreamt you met
the murdered girl, were
trying to comfort her.

It's reassuring to think
you'll go on doing
what you were good at –

but here we are road-blocked,
our walks policed or televised,
the streets subdued, until
our late-night neighbour
starts his 4 a.m. toccata –

and when I sleep again
you have your arm around her,
and you're saying, 'I know,
I had a daughter...'

On William Drummond of Hawthornden
whose fiancée died on the eve of their wedding

Well-worn paths from his beloved retreat
lead me down a hillside, scarred by storms,
to a face of rock. I can see him
where the kestrel has made a nest now –
staring across the churning river,
tracing the chisel marks above him,
holding the caves cool and comforting –
or, striding along the Esk's wild bank,
he might have opened up his anger,
conscious that he had lost forever
this first bright love. Was his grief released,
dropped hundreds of feet over the high
edge of garden? Or did it increase –
a force strong enough to uproot trees?

The Boatman's Dream

Just a boatman's dream, the kid left behind –
flicking her damp dress round the staithes, salt-stained
where she wrung the corners out. Her mouth full
of sherbet and sailors' talk, bruising words
as she flings them – Mister, giv is a fish!
Me da's run off...'
                              He throws her mackerel,
five fish at her feet. She sits to pack them
slithering into her wide blue knickers.
Some are still gasping when she starts to run
home, past men watching another tide turn –
with the promise of unfamiliar sheets
and a younger woman to kiss them warm:

masts negotiate angles they can't keep.

Intimacies

Some nights, at the top of this tall house,
I'm sitting by the window, alone,
when a light springs out across the street
in a cosy cluttered room, five floors up.
A dark figure moves across the glass:
something searched for is found – the light goes out.
A door I cannot see or hear is shut.

You won't remember that night I looked up
to catch you watching me, light in your eyes
as they searched my face. Something was found –
you seized it to store in a dark room
you never let me glimpse. I tried, but
you switched out the light whenever we talked,
and behind your eyes I heard a closing door.

Dead Books [1]

The peacock trailed his tail
in the Museum Gardens,
feathers folded on his desire.
Amongst the ruins, outside
each others' magnetic fields,
they were faithful to other people.

They should have easy minds –
yet cannot sleep, remembering
the afternoon, ruins, the museum:
illuminated pages under glass,
pronounced dead because
they couldn't be touched.

Dead Books [2]

He won't remember the incident,
she doesn't recall the place – but they
were looking at a beautiful book
in a glass case. It was sad, he said,
the way both books and people could die
if they were no longer touched with love.
She left him to stay alive.

Relate on Prospect Street

Tonight the dark thickens
with hurt women whose men
do not know they have come
to betray them – often
reluctantly, with pain.

Time and again they blame
only themselves. The walls
magnify their whispers
into accusations
without their permission.

Some have come with husbands.
Mesmerised by a light
shining through the window
they watch exhausted moths
stunning themselves senseless.

Mixed Doubles

If 'love' means 'nothing'
his smile has just caused her to
make a double fault.

This Is the House

'This is the house,' he said, 'here's a picture.'
Old brickwork, sagging roof, exposed timbers.
'The garden's wild: it's terribly quiet.
This is the house where I should like to live.'

The quiet was terrible to her, but
she learnt to survive it and the garden
compelled her to go out and dig. She thought:
'This is the house where I *should* like to live,'

but she wasn't convinced. He went to work,
envying her freedom, while she paced out
empty fields between windows, repeating:
'This is the house where I should like to *live*.'

Beyond Men

Through the shrunk boards
water strokes itself:
dives at the ends of staves.
Her eyes are out to sea:
she's gardening the waves,
weeding out boats before
they can put down roots.

Off the beach, women
bob like seals in their
round red caps – climb out,
and dance with strangers.

Under the pier, where
the sea has slipped back,
the wet sand is coldest.
It sucks her shoulders,
makes her shiver.
Arms, legs, breasts, slip
under: she struggles
out of the strong embrace.
Sleek, salt tongues of weed
lick neck and nipples –
waves return her hair
a tangle of black lace.

Dancers on the pier
drift home to their beds,
refusing late drinks
or a possessive caress.
Tonight the sea's moans
make women yearn
for something beyond
the love of men.

DIFFICULT TIMES

Sunday Prayer

Last logs burn amongst the ash.
Heaped asleep on chairs, the cats
perfect a long, controlled collapse.

Upstairs a wayward fiddle squeaks;
the beams thump to the player's feet.
Black fur flexes, stretches, sleeps.

Dust sifting through each space and fold
will settle when the doors are closed
and we are miles away from home,
the cats out hunting, music gone.

We live, trusting that house walls hold,
that we can always buy our food,
that no one takes our home away.
Forgive us our security.

God's Train

'Does God's train stop at Reading?' asked Kevin.
'Would you know God if you saw him?'
Snow blew through the waiting-room doorway.
'Has he changed his mind about resurrection?
Does he look like the Transport Police?'

Fellow passengers shivered on the platform.
When he is too cold in his room, Kevin
shuttles himself between Earley and Bracknell:
no one inspects the ticket in his shoe.
What could I say but, 'I hope so' and 'No'?

A Tale of Two Cities: 1987

Five o'clock by the Liffey: no rain all day.
Strange in my interview clothes, as bus queues grow
I find a bench, a discarded *Evening Press*:
SINGLE WOMEN thinking of religious life?
Phone Sister Eileen, Killiney 309.
I move from *Personal* to *Lost and Found*
but it's only the former – seven dogs
and a pensioner's purse on the Ballina train.

A man sits his father beside me while he
reads his paper. I take in a few prayers:
St Jude worker of miracles pray for us
St Jude helper of the hopeless pray for us
Say 9 times a day for 9 days – M.T.
The old man moves his coat and, for a second,
I think he's playing with a hamster until,
with 'Holy Mother!', his son buttons him up.
He smiles and I smile back.

The bridges are full of people begging.
In O'Connell Street I am stopped four times
by women without coats, whose bare arms
are pale as their voices, half-heartedly asking.
I don't have enough of the right kind of money.
All afternoon I've wandered from Park to Gallery,
a London return ticket in my pocket.
Until I met them I was content, but now,
seeing a girl lie down with her baby
on the steps of a crumbling Georgian facade,
I'm more aware of my first-time-on jacket,
of the books and dreams which set us apart.

The sun is catching the windscreens of buses.
Outside the Abbey Theatre an old girl
takes my arm: 'Will ye look at that!' She points –
photographs – an actress hitching up her skirts.
She laughs and shakes her head and laughs again –
'Will ye look at that!' We look. She wanders off.

As it grows dark I ask my way through littered streets.
Like a relay team, one by one, my guides
lead me on until our paths part. No one
coldly points a finger down a road, or offers
meaningless directions, or says that they don't know.
On the bus leaving Dublin a woman
asks why I came: 'Sure, there's no work here.' Yet
I'd been invited to try my luck – was sent
a free ticket. 'If they asked you, there'd be
no one here could do it.' She suddenly approved:
'You'll read a lot?' I don't meself. It turned out
she was almost blind. On the seat beside her
I left my paper – open at the page:
To St Jude in thanksgiving for favour received.

In the end, her first thought proved the right one.
Money was short everywhere, not just on the streets.
These days, in tube stations and tourist spots
I see them – single women of the new religion:
no coats, cheap clothes, shadowed eyes. A quiet voice
at your elbow as busy roads cross, a woman
by the railings outside the British Museum – where
fifty pence buys you a bead for good luck
based on some ancient charm – or, with arms full of books,
you can put the coin in her hand and walk away.

Gulf

When I wake alone in a drone of planes
it's twenty to five – three nights since you left,
just noise in the sky over someone's roof
as they tried to sleep. These pass, heading east,
their high whine muffled by thousands of feet.
I've dreamt of men, whose minds are drifting sand,
guiding you to airstrips on unknown ground.
In the glare of my lamp dust swirls and gleams,
sticks in my throat as I reach for a drink.
Tomorrow news will flash on TV screens
and, in the moment I'm not looking, you'll
be seen – acting as normal, as if all
this could be over soon – but then my glass
hits the table; it echoes round the room.

Difficult Times

These are difficult times. April arrived
through a rush of rain. In the train window
a newspaper – fingers at either side –
skimmed, superimposed, across a landscape
bereft of houses. A child's charred hand dropped
out of focus – emerged from a long
pool of waste water and was folded up,
left on the seat.
              We are watching this war
on a faraway screen without the sound.
Nothing seems to matter more than the rain.
As we left that train the city filled with
workers and shoppers, doing whatever
passes for life.
             The value of pity
sinks slowly in our purses and pockets;
we edge along pavements. In a minute,
someone anywhere might be blown to pieces:
it's all either cowardice or courage.
Daily, new mothers are wielding pushchairs,
thrusting their offspring out, ahead of them,
into the face of oncoming traffic.

Underground Rap

They dance below the moving stairs;
trains rattle off to Leicester Square.
Their furious feet attack the ground;
a drunk man staggers and sits down,
the cello player starts to play
around the corner.
                              A woman sways
on scraping heels, her briefcase
knocking at her knees. She squeezes
through the coated backs,
                              drops a coin.
They DANCE.
Shirts belly with the funnelled breeze,
the feet swing out, the dreadlocks leap.
We go to Goodge Street.
                              In the lift,
a bare room where two vast walls shift,
twisting a neck towards scarred arms,
a man in a shrunken T-shirt turns
his face away.
                              His skin is stained
with cold – and punctured, messed-up veins.
Much later, he still hasn't moved –
just up and down, as if he's trapped
to ferry out of hell and back.
At Waterloo the homeless sit
as silent as the river's drift.
Fast taxis sweep their dark suits past;
the brand new cars, the money, pass.
A stage-door closes.
                              Over there
a blanket struggles up some stairs
and huddles, holding out a card
while feet avoid it in the dark
and rush to reach the Circle Bar.
Ten minutes till the play begins
a wily theatre critic skims
his practised eye across the programme.

Two soup runs start.
                    The players fight:
it's kill or be killed here tonight –
they die, as actors sometimes do.
The critic makes a note or two,
then hurries back to Waterloo
above a cast of people who
stage nothing, just live in full view.

Whistler with Two Coats

Every night he catches the wind
on a bridge above passing trains;
staves it off with two thin coats, shirts,
his skin. Quaver lures breve into
cold spaces beside the river,
nocturne without gold: still figure.

Exchange notes with him. The second
his cut-glove fingers touch your sleeve,
it plays back warmth he cannot keep.
For like these others hurrying past,
we wear one ample coat which fits,
to fix us mute, in blue: in black.

Metaphor
(for Mary Feddon and Strawberry Hill)

At first we didn't notice it was growing dark.
We lit the chandeliers at noon – then earlier.
Sometimes we tripped over furniture:
the gloom cast up a suit of armour.
Each one of us felt the cold iron hand
on our shoulder, some time or other,
crept our way down corridors
which were growing narrower.

Yet it was broad day by the gazebo. Birds sang.
The garden stretched out in the sun
like a woman reclining on a long, curved couch.
Inside, we stumbled, losing our grip on the light.
We saw that this darkness was special to us.
Doorways filled and shrank with shadows.
Sometimes voices called across the tiles
tempting us to jump over the castled edge.

We turned our backs. Then one day
a harlequin ran towards the house.
Clowns bounced down the lawns. Their music
lured a few of us out – for a moment or two.
Not all made it back. (Notice the girl
blowing by the border; the dog, still trying
to leap out of his shape.) We couldn't escape
except back to the dark. Nowhere was safe.

The music took squirrels into the river:
a peacock span round on the highest turret
and disappeared – but indoor, books rustled,
there were glimmers of light: there were the hands.
Hands on the stair-rail below the Library –
ordinary hands with the touch of a mother,
moving together; folding the dark
into long, heavy sheets, corner to corner.

They were all the magic that we knew
against darkness. They shook out shadows.
Gradually we learnt to hear our own music;
learnt to distrust the slick sparkle of clowns.

Replay

She drove him wild as a child when she
crashed through his silence – he lay in bed
recovering from flu. Her mother
was out, nursing '*really* sick people'
and there wasn't a great deal he could
be bothered to do – especially when
she asked a lot of daft questions and
insisted he repeat the same mad
tale till she was telling it for him,
over and over. He could hardly
raise his head to look at the paper:
all he wanted was to lie and sleep.

Sitting by her bed ten years later
he is silent, replaying the same
crazy sequence of squeals, bang, and slow
trickling glass. Her mother never
comes now – she can't bear it, but he
stays, asking ridiculous questions
day after day, till he knows each one
by heart. Sometimes he will remember –
in the desperate sunshine – and slump
over her hand; can't raise his eyes.
A nurse will bring him in a paper,
try to be cheerful. She drives him wild.

The Destruction of Sodom and Gomorrah

(from the painting by John Martin, 1852)

No one ever asks why I looked back.
They all know the story of Lot's wife
who stood stupidly despairing when
she should have fled. It was not like that.

Imagine a great tide of fire
with waves higher than nearby mountains
crashing down, at once, on two cities –
buildings, bodies exploding. The heat.

I breathed in spray of freshly-burnt flesh:
friends, neighbours – my young, married daughters
whose husbands would not heed Lot's warnings.
I'd wanted them to marry herdsmen...

Yet Lot was always a city man,
tolerating our city's ways till
its rabble threatened to rape his guests.
His response? 'Leave them: take my daughters.'

We still had two girls waiting marriage:
'They have not known man; do as you will,
only spare these men under my roof.'
Luckily the strangers intervened –

but after that I would rather have
fed myself to the raging furnace
than follow him. The sun was rising:
eventually I had little choice.

We were out before flames closed the gates,
welded them into the scorching stones:
the sun, smothered in fumes. No strangers
to be seen – only a burning sea

vaporising. I could taste the salt,
feel it crust my fingers; the muscles
of my face tightened. It stung my eyes.
As towers toppled, I became one.

Salt corrodes but I would rather watch
destruction than follow my children
to a desperate future, plying
their father with wine from Gomorrah

until he lies senseless and they claim
his wizened body as their birthright,
taking turns at my place in his bed,
handling him, taking his seed by force –

I noticed the pitchers carried *so*
carefully, the wild plans in their eyes
as he herded them past me. I could
not bear to face the future. Looked back.

Pandora's Daughter

I have kept a spoon
licked by the last woman
to run from the kitchen
when lava leered through a doorway
in lonely Pompey.

I keep all deserted ruins,
abandoned homes,
unanswered prayers.

My box is hinged with sighs.
It expands in the dark
to cover continents.
It shrinks at morning
so you can put it on a shelf
or even in your pocket –
but never in someone else's:
it is always heavy.

I open it constantly,
add sorrow by the shovelful:
the man who married someone else,
the woman who sacrificed herself,
the children who were never born –
all buried under a thousand wars,
millions of unfed mouths,
an avalanche of frozen tears.

I sift them with this spoon
(it is large, like a ladle),
and wish that I could alter
reality to fable;
that I could lose
box and spoon together;

that I could
forgive my mother.

Rock

The rock had spent thousands of years
on the spot where he had tumbled
when the glacier left him.
The tiny fissure in the earth at his base
became bigger: water seeped into it –
it widened and followed its own course.
The rock watched, always from the same spot.

Men came and went. The rock watched.
He grew tired, weak, felt that every storm
was wearing him down. Even the red ants
were dismantling him, grain by grain.
He had broken himself into boulders
and let them roll away: lichen, thrift,
wagtails' feet persisted. He stopped caring.

One day a woman appeared, gathering ling
and bilberries. The rock saw her, struggling
in the bushes with bedding, brooms, fruit
for her children. She sensed his dilemma,
drew closer, laid her hand against rock,
and passed on her power. 'Endure,'
she said – and the rock endured.

NOTES

Kith *(page 11)*
In 1138, David I, King of the Scots, moved the Scottish border down to the Eden and the Tees so that the country was divided into almost two equal parts. At one time Northumbria stretched as far as the Firth of Forth and Cumberland was part of the Celtic kingdom of Strathclyde. For much of the 11th century Northumbria alternated between Scotland and England and Scottish kings paid homage for Tynedale intermittently for two more centuries. The present border dates from the 13th century.

Gruoch *(page 17)*
Gruoch was directly descended from Kenneth III of Scotland (murdered by Malcolm II to secure the throne for his grandson, Duncan). She married Macbeth *c.*1032, either when she was pregnant with her son (Lulach) by her first partner, Gillecomgain, or soon after his birth. Lulach succeeded to the throne in August 1057 on the death of Macbeth (who slew Duncan and was, in turn, killed by Duncan's son, another Malcolm). In *Gruoch Considers*, having taken stock of her situation, she argues herself into the second marriage with Macbeth.

Ullambana *(pages 24-5)*
Ullambana is a Buddhist festival for the remembrance of the dead and the liberation of unquiet spirits. On this night the souls of the dead return to their former homes to be honoured by their descendants.

Mariamne Johnes of Hafod *(pages 30-1)*
Mariamne died in 1811 but the magnificent memorial commissioned by her father, Thomas Johnes, from Sir Francis Chantrey stayed in the latter's studio till the Duke of Newcastle paid for it and installed it at Eglwys Newydd in 1832. Thomas Johnes died in 1816 and both he and Mariamne are buried in the Chancel vault. The memorial was destroyed by fire in 1932 – 125 years after flames swept through Johnes' original Gothic mansion. Hafod lies in the Ystwyth Valley.

Transliteration *(page 32)*
заканчивать (pronounced 'zakánchivat') means 'end, complete, conclude'; страшный (pronounced 'strashni') means 'terrible, dreadful'. Mandelstam's poem referred to in the second stanza is '*No, not the moon, but the bright clock-face*', from *Stone* (1912), translated by James Greene in *The Eyesight of Wasps* (Angel Books, 1989).